Shep

Our Most Loyal Dog

Sneed B. Collard III

Illustrated by Joanna Yardley

To my first dog, Puppy, who shared my wandering spirit.

—Sneed

For Osa, Jammy, and Charlie and all those loyal
pets and friends we have all had.

—Joanna

Thanks to the Schwinden Library & Archives in Fort Benton,
Montana and the *Great Falls Tribune.* *—J.Y.*

Text Copyright © 2006 Sneed B. Collard
Illustration Copyright © 2006 Joanna Yardley

All rights reserved. No part of this book may be reproduced in any
manner without the express written consent of the publisher. All
inquiries should be addressed to:

Sleeping Bear Press
310 North Main Street, Suite 300
Chelsea, MI 48118
www.sleepingbearpress.com

THOMSON
GALE

© 2006 Thomson Gale, a part of the Thomson Corporation.

Thomson, Star Logo and Sleeping Bear Press are trademarks
and Gale is a registered trademark used herein under license.

Printed and bound in China.
First Edition
10 9 8 7 6 5 4 3 2 1

Library of Congress
Cataloging-in-Publication Data

Collard, Sneed B.
Shep : our most loyal dog / written by Sneed B.
Collard III;
illustrated by Joanna Yardley.
p. cm.
Summary: "This is the true story of a Montana dog who became a worldwide
inspiration. In 1936, Shep watched as his master's body was placed on a train and
shipped east. For more than five years Shep met every incoming train with hopes
that he would see the man who had cared for him"—Provided by publisher.
ISBN 1-58536-259-X
1. Shep (Dog) 2. Collie—Montana—Fort Benton—Biography. 3. Sheep dogs—
Montana—Fort Benton—Biography. I. Title.

SF429.C6C55 2006
636.737'4—dc22   2005027656

The shrill whistle of a steam locomotive pierced the air and a passenger train thundered toward the station.

The sheep dog looked on as several men removed a long, rough-cut wooden box from the back of a hearse and rolled it across the platform. As the men heaved the wooden box into the train's baggage car, the dog began to whine.

Few people noticed.

The baggage car doors slammed shut and the locomotive's whistle shrieked. Then, with a loud hiss of steam and the labored panting of a thousand horses, the train slowly chugged east into the shadows cast by the afternoon sun.

Sad and confused, the sheep dog watched it go. It was the first of thousands of trains the dog would watch leave the station over the next five and a half years. It was also the beginning of one of the greatest chapters in the history of dogs and men—the story of the dog simply known as "Shep."

Shep was born in the sweeping cattle and sheep country of north central Montana, probably in the late 1920s. Every spring, his Master loaded up a sheep wagon and he and the dog headed out into grazing country with a great white flock. During the long Montana days, Shep raced joyously back and forth, barking at the sheep to steer them toward fresh grass. He kept a keen lookout for rattlesnakes and coyotes and rounded up any woolies that wandered away.

At night, when the sheep were settled down, Shep curled up at his Master's feet next to the campfire. His Master stroked Shep's fur and hummed a soft tune. Shep let out a deep, contented sigh. Soon, his paws began to twitch as he dreamed about another

Through thousands of days and nights, the bond between man and dog grew. One summer, though, when Shep was perhaps six or seven years old, his Master fell ill. Shep had watched his Master get sick before. Sometimes, the man coughed or slept more than usual. Soon, though, he'd be up and around, back to his normal self.

Not this time.

As days passed, his Master grew worse. One day, a horse-drawn "buckboard" came out to the sheep wagon. Two strangers lifted his Master into the buckboard and drove away. Shep followed along behind.

The buckboard drove over rough country roads until it reached the town of Fort Benton on the Missouri River. The roar of car engines and shouts of people frightened Shep. He grew even more alarmed when the buckboard stopped and the men carried his Master into a large, wooden building. Shep tried to follow, but women in strange, starched uniforms kept him out.

For the next several days Shep waited anxiously outside the hospital. He wasn't the only one waiting. These were the years of the Great Depression. All over the country, millions of people were out of work and homeless. Down-on-their-luck hobos, or drifters, often passed through Fort Benton. They waited at the back of the hospital for a large woman named Sister Genevieve to come out and serve them a hot meal. Noticing the anxious shepherd dog nearby, Sister Genevieve also began setting out scraps of food and water for Shep.

Shep probably expected his Master to come walking out of the hospital at any time, but he never did. Instead, the illness took his Master's life. A day or two later, a hearse carried Shep's Master to the Great Northern Railway depot so that it could be shipped to relatives back east.

As he watched the train disappear around a bend, Shep probably didn't realize he was saying goodbye.

And so began the great wait.

From that day forward, Shep met every passenger train that arrived at the Fort Benton depot. As passengers from all over the world disembarked, Shep studied each face and caught every scent, searching for his Master. Sometimes, a kindly man or woman tried to pet him, but Shep backed off. When the train again chugged and huffed into the distance, the shepherd dog also disappeared.

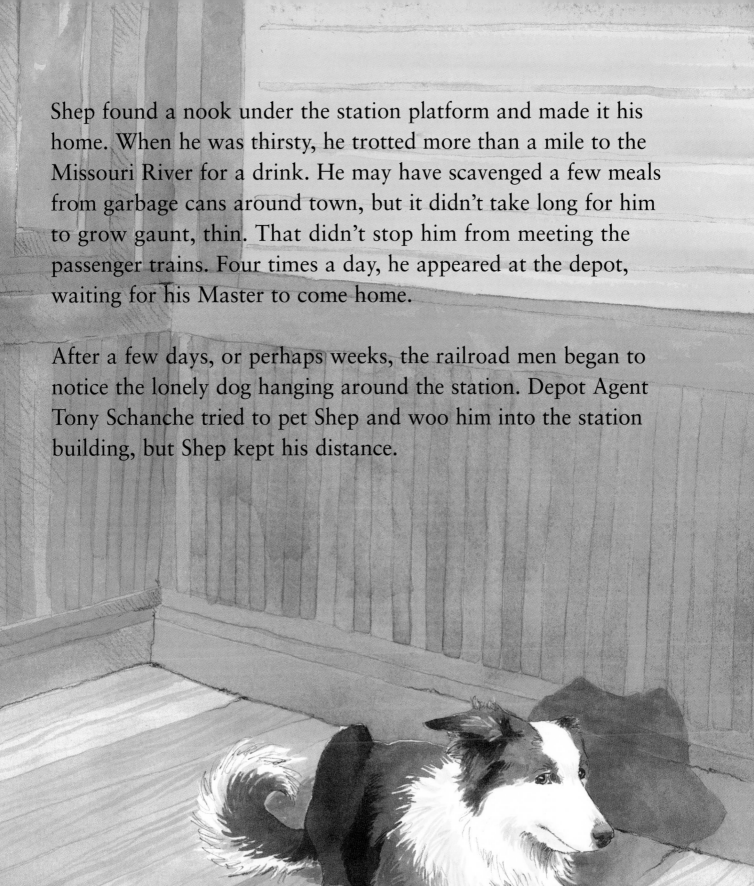

Shep found a nook under the station platform and made it his home. When he was thirsty, he trotted more than a mile to the Missouri River for a drink. He may have scavenged a few meals from garbage cans around town, but it didn't take long for him to grow gaunt, thin. That didn't stop him from meeting the passenger trains. Four times a day, he appeared at the depot, waiting for his Master to come home.

After a few days, or perhaps weeks, the railroad men began to notice the lonely dog hanging around the station. Depot Agent Tony Schanche tried to pet Shep and woo him into the station building, but Shep kept his distance.

Steve McSweeney, whose dad Pat was a section foreman, also noticed the dog. Not long after Shep showed up, Steve and his mom Kitty started walking to the depot with table scraps and water for Shep. After setting down the food, they hid and watched to see what the dog would do. At first, Shep just sniffed the food and left it alone. Soon, though, his hunger overcame his suspicions and he began eating the offerings.

But no one could replace Shep's Master. When Steve or Kitty or one of the station hands tried to pet the dog, he shied away and disappeared until the next passenger train rolled in. The McSweeneys didn't give up. They kept bringing food and water and, after six or seven weeks, Shep finally let Steve and Kitty pet him. Tony Schanche again tried to coax Shep into the depot building to sleep, but the dog would have none of it. He still preferred his nook under the platform.

As winter set in, however, and temperatures plunged toward zero, Shep found it harder and harder to resist the warmth of the station house. One evening, Tony set some scraps of meat inside the depot and Shep cautiously stepped in. He looked carefully around him and sniffed the air for danger. Then, he walked over to the meat and gulped it down.

When the door closed behind him, though, Shep panicked. Terrified, he raced around the depot, overturning furniture, frantically looking for a way out. Tony moved slowly and spoke soothingly. Finally, after many minutes, Shep calmed down. From then on, Shep began spending his nights on a comfortable bed of blankets.

All this time, Tony and the McSweeneys had no idea where Shep came from or why he hung around the station. They didn't even know the dog's real name. A conductor named Ed Shields, though, began asking people if they knew who the dog might be.

One day, Ed climbed down to help passengers off the train and asked a nearby railroad worker if he knew anything about the dog.

"Oh," the worker replied, "he belonged to a sheep-herder who died. They shipped his body away and that dog has been hanging around ever since."

Over the next two years, Ed talked to Fort Benton's undertaker and many others about Shep. He slowly untangled the story of how Shep had come to Fort Benton and why he met the trains. Ed reported his findings to the *Great Falls Tribune* and the newspaper ran a story about the lonesome shepherd dog. From then on, Shep's legend began to grow.

Shep's story streaked across America. Newspapers all over the country picked up the plight of the loyal dog who waited for his Master. His name even crossed the oceans to Europe and Australia. Men, women, and children wrote hundreds of letters to the Great Northern Railway—so many that the company had to assign a secretary to handle them all. People sent money to help care for Shep. One woman from England even sent Shep a bone and a cake made of suet.

But people didn't just write letters. Hundreds started traveling to Fort Benton to catch a glimpse of the famous shepherd dog. More than fifty sheepherders offered to give Shep a new home herding sheep. Some even came in person to take the dog home. Tony Schanche politely refused the offers.

Shep didn't seem to think much of all the attention. The clicking cameras scared him. Besides, even though he continued to wait for his Master, Shep now had a good life. His conductor friend Ed brought him snacks whenever he passed through Fort Benton, and Tony Schanche treated Shep like royalty. Tony loved sweets and often slipped the dog a flavored LifeSaver candy. In between passenger trains, Shep curled up at Tony's feet as he had once done with his Master.

On December 7th, 1941, Japanese forces attacked the United States naval base at Pearl Harbor. Within days, the United States entered World War II and streams of soldiers traveled the trains through Fort Benton. By this time, Shep had grown old. He was no longer quick on his feet and his hearing had begun to desert him.

One cold January morning, Shep wandered out onto the railroad tracks to gnaw on a bone that was stuck there. As he worked the bone, the westbound 235 train approached the station. The engineer spotted the dog on the tracks and blasted the whistle. Shep kept chewing his bone. The engine whistle again blew, but Shep didn't move. Only a few yards from the dog, the engineer threw on all of its brakes but it was too late.

Steve's mom Kitty walked down the hill to the Fort Benton school to tell Steve about Shep's death. Steve and the other school children were devastated. Word of the tragedy swept through town and everywhere, people cried over the loss of their beloved dog.

The city fathers and men of the Great Northern Railway decided to hold a funeral for Shep. Tony stayed up most of the night building a wooden coffin.

On Wednesday afternoon, two days after Shep's death, hundreds of people arrived in cars and buses and gathered next to the airport road above the Fort Benton depot. A warm Chinook wind had melted the snow, and the winter sun sparkled as four Boy Scouts carried Shep to the gravesite overlooking the station.

As the mourners wiped their eyes and hugged each other, Reverend Ralph Underwood read "Eulogy on the Dog" by Senator George Graham Vest:

> *The one absolutely unselfish friend that man can
> have in this selfish world, the one that never deserts
> him, the one that never proves ungrateful
> or treacherous, is his dog…*

When the service ended, a lone Boy Scout raised his bugle and blew a slow, mournful taps.

Epilogue

News wires delivered the sad news of Shep's death all over the country and the world. Everywhere, people remembered and talked about the faithful shepherd dog. But Shep's story didn't fade away.

In the years that followed, magazine articles about Shep appeared in Reader's Digest, Lady's Circle, *and* Farm Journal. *People from far and wide traveled to Fort Benton to leave flowers and pay their respects.*

Shep's legacy lives on today. If you ever are lucky enough to visit Fort Benton, take a few minutes to drive up the hill to the train depot. Passenger trains no longer pass through and the old depot has long since been torn down and replaced by a smaller, simpler building. But if you stand and look up the hill, you will see a concrete tombstone and the name "SHEP"—reminders of the remarkable dog who taught us what loyalty and heart are all about.

～ Telling Shep's Story ～

I first got to know Shep while writing my book *B is for Big Sky Country: A Montana Alphabet*. The book focuses on Montana people, places, nature, and history and I chose Shep to represent the letter "S." When the book was published, readers asked me so many questions about Shep, I knew I needed to write a more complete story about him.

Over the years, Shep's tale has been told hundreds of times—always with passion if not 100% accuracy! To separate fact from fiction, I pored over dozens of magazine and newspaper articles, letters, photographs, and booklets. These were provided by Henry Armstrong, Kenneth Robison, and Donna Wahlberg at the River and Plains Museum in Fort Benton.

I was also fortunate enough to be able to interview three people who knew Shep firsthand: Steve McSweeney; John, or "Jack," Lepley (a pallbearer at Shep's funeral and author of a terrific booklet on Shep); and the daughter of Tony Schanche, Irene Bowker. I am deeply indebted to these people for providing me with details and perspective on Shep's life.

Finally, I visited Fort Benton to see and experience Shep's world for myself. From this research I tried to create the most honest account possible given the resources available and the many years that have passed since Shep's death. My artistic license comes into play only during Shep's unknown early years before his Master died. Here, I was forced to try to reconstruct what a sheepherder's and shepherd dog's life might have been like in Montana during the 1920s and '30s. I am sure that my story will not satisfy everyone and to those people I apologize, but please know I have done my best to stay true to Shep and his life.

By the way, one common question about Shep is "What did his Master die from?" No one knows for sure, but from accounts I have read, it seems likely that the man died of tuberculosis, a common killer of the day.

An even greater mystery is "Who was Shep's Master?" Remarkably, his identity still eludes us. Several sheepherders died in the summer of 1936, but no one has ever been able to pinpoint which one was Shep's Master. Perhaps one of the readers of this book will be inspired to search anew for an answer.

Readers will be pleased to know that, more than fifty years after his death, Shep remains a beloved figure in Montana and throughout the West. On June 26th, 1994, Fort Benton's city fathers unveiled a new bronze statue to honor their famous dog. Today, if you visit downtown Fort Benton, you can see the handsome bronze memorial, surrounded by bricks with messages from hundreds of well-wishers.